Centered Christmas

Christmas: A December Daily Heart Companion

Copyright (c) 2022 by Kirstin J. Ricketts

All rights reserved. No part of this publication may be reproduced or transmitted in any form by any means, electronic, mechanical, photocopy, recording or otherwise without the prior permission of the publisher, except as provided for by the USA copyright law.

All Scripture quotations, unless otherwise indicated, are taken from the Holy Bible, New International Version®, NIV®. Copyright ©1973, 1978, 1984, 2011 by Biblica, Inc.™ Used by permission of Zondervan. All rights reserved worldwide www.zondervan.com. The "NIV" and "New International Version" are trademarks registered in the United States Patent and Trademark Office by Biblica, Inc.™

Scripture quotations marked (ESV) are taken from the Holy Bible, English Standard Version, copyright © 2001 by Crossway, a publishing ministry of Good News Publishers. All rights reserved.

Scripture quotations marked (NLT) are taken from the Holy Bible, New Living Translation, copyright ©1996, 2004, 2015 by Tyndale House Foundation. Used by permission of Tyndale House Publishers, Carol Stream, Illinois 60188. All rights reserved.

Adams, Charles Adolphe. O Holy Night. PD, 1847. Edited by Michael Kravchuk.
https://michaelkravchuk.com/wp-content/uploads/2017/02/O-Holy-Night-Bb-Major.pdf.

Anonymous. God Rest Ye Merry Gentlemen. PD, 1927. Edited by Michael Kravchuk.
https://michaelkravchuk.com/wp-content/uploads/2017/03/God-Rest-You-Merry-Gentlemen-Full-Score.pdf.

Mohr, Joseph. Silent Night. PD, 1818. Edited by Michael Kravchuk.
https://michaelkravchuk.com/wp-content/uploads/2017/02/Silent-Night-Bb-Major.pdf.

Watts, Isaac. Joy to the World. PD, 1836. Edited by Michael Kravchuk.
https://michaelkravchuk.com/wp-content/uploads/2019/12/Joy-To-The-World-D-Major-1.pdf.

Preparing for His Arrival

Jesus is King. He is the Messiah, the Son of God sent to earth to redeem the world. To redeem you and to redeem me. He was Lord from first breath. This December, let's breathe deeply and relish in the season.

Let's let God recapture His place in our hearts and in our lives. Let's be crafted into worshipers compelled by love's pure light. This December, let's receive Jesus as King.

Before we begin: Write God a letter asking Him for the desire to make Jesus the King of your heart this Holiday Season.

Joy to the World

arranged by Andriy Makarevych

December 1
Joy to the world! The Lord is come.

He has come. If you asked a child if Jesus has come, their wide eyes would say, "Of course! He is in the manger in my neighbor's yard!" We see these scenes popping up, but do we live like the Lord has come? Does it give us great joy? Our Savior was born in a stable. He has saved us and He is coming again. God, let that bring us great joy.

For reflection - Am I living with the realization that for thousands of years, there was a promise written in the Scriptures and it has been fulfilled by the coming of Jesus our Messiah? God, sew this truth into my heart today.

Write to God below -

✝

Luke 2:11 Today in the town of David a Savior has been born to you; he is the Messiah, the Lord.

December 2

Let earth receive her King.

Receive. Many things are courting our affections. Although the hope of Christmas is right in front of us, have we let it settle in? To receive our King, we must turn our hearts from the things we have made king. Today let's turn and receive.

For reflection - What does your heart turn towards? What have you made king? What are we worshiping rather than our Savior? Let's ask God to help us turn our hearts and receive the only true King.

Write to God below -

2 Timothy 2:22 Flee the evil desires of youth and pursue righteousness, faith, love and peace, along with those who call on the Lord out of a pure heart.

December 3

Let every heart prepare Him room.

Make Room. We make room for holiday fun, but have we made time to consider the hope we have in Jesus our Savior? To receive, we must make room. Set a five minute timer, let your heart come to slow and prepare Him room with this in mind, "I am preparing Him room."

For reflection - In the pause, how did God lead your heart to receive? Write to God asking Him to help you receive Jesus as your King this season.

Write to God below -

Psalm 46:10 Be still, and know that I am God.

December 4

And heaven and nature sing.

And heaven and nature sing. Praise. Look around at the trees today. Notice the birds. Notice the sunrise. Do you see it? Can you hear it? Heaven and nature are singing. Capture those sounds and images in your mind and imagine the beauty bringing great glory to Jesus our King. Praise Him with them.

For reflection - Let's bring God our gift of praise today. God, I hear You in the _____. God, I praise You like the _____. God stir our hearts to sing.

Write to God below -

Hebrews 13:15-16 Through Jesus, therefore, let us continually offer to God a sacrifice of praise-the fruit of lips that openly profess his name. And do not forget to do good and to share with others, for with such sacrifices God is pleased.

December 5

Joy to the world! The Savior reigns.
Let men their songs employ.

Be His instrument. To employ means to use. When we know who and whose we are, our voice can be an instrument of our Father's. This could be as simple as life-giving words or as complicated as proclaiming the gospel to the nations. Whatever God tells your instrument to do, let's remember to let Him fill us, His vessel, and employ.

For reflection - How is your voice an instrument of God's? Is it repeating the sounding joy? Ask God how He would like your voice to be an instrument for His use.

Write to God below -

Psalm 19:14 May these words of my mouth and this meditation of my heart be pleasing in your sight, LORD, my Rock and my Redeemer.

December 6

He rules the world with truth and grace.

God, I believe You. I have to remind myself, not only do I believe in God, but I believe what He says. I believe Him. Sometimes this flows effortlessly and other times, for all of us, we must choose to believe God. "God I believe You rule the world and that You do so with truth and grace. Your promises are true and as Your child I live with Your face of favor shining upon my face." Imagine the sun rising and reflecting upon someone's face. Now imagine it is you, and the light is the favor of God. Hold that closely today.

For reflection - Who does God say He is? Write a list of "God You are _____." Do you believe Him? Let's ask God to help us believe Him.

Write to God below -

Mark 9:24 "I do believe; help me overcome my unbelief!"

December 7

And glories of His righteousness & wonders of His Love.

Wonder. When my heart is in the healthiest space, I begin to wonder. I wonder at God showing His love and kindness. I see His great love towards His children, those who believe all over the earth. If God's kindness is difficult to see, that's okay. God can handle all of our feelings. It's okay to say, "God, today I can't see Your kindness. As I proceed, let me wonder at Your great love."

For reflection - Sit with God. Ask Him to reveal to you places in your life where He is providing and showing kindness. Write Him a letter of gratitude and ask Him to stir wonder at His love. If kindness is difficult for you to see, tell Him about that too. Wait and see what He says.

Write to God below -

Psalm 86:13 For great is your love toward me;
you have delivered me from the depths, from the realm of the dead.

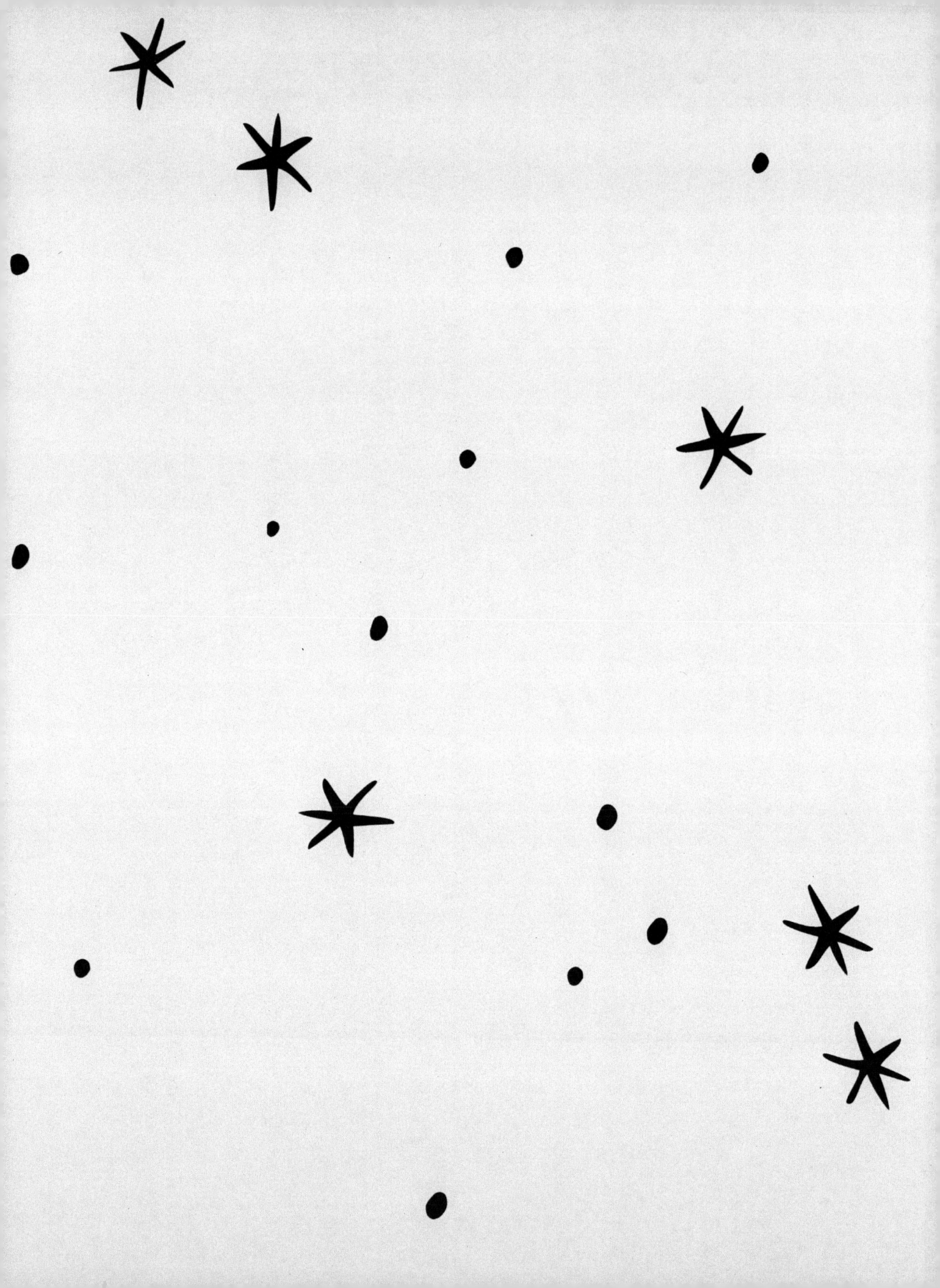

God Rest Ye Merry Gentlemen

God rest ye mer-ry, gen-tle-men, let no-thing you dis-may, Re-mem-ber, Christ our Sa-vior was born on Christ-mas day. To save us all from Sa-tan's pow'r when we were gone a-stray, O____

From God out Heav'nly Fa-ther a bles-sed An-gel came, And un-to cer-tain Shep-herds brought ti-dings of the same: How that in Beth-le-hem was born the Son of God by Name,

"Fear not then," said the An-gel, "Let no-thing you a-fright, This day is born a Sa-vior a bles-sed ho-ly sight, To free all those who trust in Him from Sa-tan's pow'r and might."

Now to the Lord sing pra-ises, all you with-in this place, And with true love and bro-ther-hood each o-ther now em-brace; This Ho-ly Child of Christ-mas shall fill our hearts with grace:

ti-dings of com-fort and joy, Com-fort and joy O____ ti-dings of com-fort and joy.

©MichaelKravchuk.com

December 8

God rest.

Come close. "God rest" means "rest assured," like a father would pull his child in close and whisper to her, "Rest assured. Let nothing steal your gaze." Let God pull you in close. "Rest assured. Rest assured, I will teach you. Rest assured, I will craft you. Rest assured, I will provide for you. Rest assured, I will protect you. Rest assured, I sent my Son to be the Savior of the world."

For reflection - What is God inviting you to rest in with Him today?
Fill in the blank: Rest assured, _____ .

Write to God below -

James 4:8 Come near to God and he will come near to you.

December 9

Ye merry gentlemen.

Mighty and Joyful. There is some dispute on whether the merry here means mighty or joyful, but as daughters of the King, we are both. Whether you feel it or not, in Him you are mighty and in Him you can have great joy. Our strength isn't our own and lasting joy won't come from the decor we place around our homes. Our joy will come from the Lord, the maker of heaven and earth. Close your eyes and picture yourself being fully supplied with His strength and joy. In Him you are mighty and joyful.

For reflection - What are you looking to for your strength? What are you looking to for your joy? Make a list and return those things to God. Ask Him to be the source of your joy and strength.

Write to God below -

Psalm 121:1-2 I lift up my eyes to the mountains -
where does my help come from?
My help comes from the LORD, the Maker of heaven and earth.

December 10

Let nothing you dismay.

We can talk with God. Dismay is a total loss of courage. Our worries and fears can feel big. Sometimes they feel too big to carry. We may feel defeated. We can bring these things to God, and as we do, we may find His voice sounds different than we expected. Our loving Father doesn't expect us to enter the holiday season and cover our feelings with smells of peppermint and cheap ribbon. He invites us to come and sit with Him. As we do, there we will find comfort and joy.

For reflection - What is God inviting you to sit in with Him today? What fear is God inviting you to bring Him? Once when I said, "God, this makes me so sad," His reply was, "It makes me sad too." Now that is comfort and joy.

Write to God below -

Isaiah 41:10 So do not fear, for I am with you; do not be dismayed, for I am your God. I will strengthen you and help you; I will uphold you with my righteous right hand.

December 11

Remember, Christ our Savior was born on Christmas Day.

Don't forget to remember. In the hustle and bustle of the preparations, we can forget to remember. Let's spend some time remembering. Remember the young virgin who received a message from God through an angel that she would give birth to the Messiah. Remember how the shepherds returned to their fields glorifying and praising God because it was just as they had been told. Remember how Mary treasured these things in her heart. Spend some time treasuring them too.

For reflection - Ask God for eyes to see. Make a list of the events of the Christmas story. Is there a theme to your list? Ask God if there is something more He is inviting you to see, remember and treasure in His story.

Write to God below -

Luke 2:19-20 But Mary treasured up all these things and pondered them in her heart. The shepherds returned, glorifying and praising God for all the things they had heard and seen, which were just as they had been told.

December 12

To save us all from Satan's pow'r when we were gone astray.

Redemption. Ultimately, we were "gone astray." My heart continues to go astray. Let us remember if we are children of God, we have ultimately been saved from Satan's power. As children of God we are redeemed. When God sees us, He sees His Son's sacrifice, and it is enough. We have been saved from satan's power when we were gone astray.

For reflection - Sit with God. Ask Him to bring to mind a time when you went astray. Picture Jesus' blood covering that situation and yourself leaving redeemed, set free. Who were you before you were redeemed? What have you been saved from? What sort of life does God invite you into now?

Write to God below - .

Isaiah 53:6 We all, like sheep, have gone astray, each of us has turned to our own way; and the LORD has laid on him the iniquity of us all.

December 13

Oh tidings.

There is good news. What message are you putting out into the world? Sometimes, the news I am bringing is fear and anxiety. When the Holy Spirit flows through us, we can bring the fruit of the Spirit. Breathe out. Ask God to rid your heart of the things that are not from Him. Breathe in deeply. Picture the Holy Spirit filling you and pushing out anxiety, fear or whatever God leads you to let go of. Picture Him now replacing those things. As you enter into today, picture yourself bringing good news. God, would You bring us Your good news, and would You bring others good news through us.

For reflection - What message is your life putting out into the world? What is God inviting you to let Him replace? Ask God to rid your heart of those things and replace them with the fruit of the Spirit.

Write to God below -

Galatians 5:22-23 But the fruit of the Spirit is love, joy, peace, patience, kindness, goodness, faithfulness, gentleness, self-control. (ESV)

December 14

Comfort and joy.

God bestows what our hearts seek. Comfort and joy. Isn't that what we often seek as we decorate our homes for the holidays? We all want comfort and joy. What will we do to get them? Comfort and joy come in lasting ways solely from the Father. Picture your favorite Christmas decor or smell. What about it reminds you of comfort and joy? Sit in the stillness and picture being endlessly supplied with comfort and joy. As daughters of the King we are fully supplied with comfort and joy by our Heavenly Father. God, would the smells of the season that feel like home remind us we are always at home in You. Would You feel more like comfort and joy than the smell of holiday treats. Wrap us in Your love, surround us with Your Presence. Bring us comfort and joy.

For reflection - What Christmas smells or decor bring you comfort and joy? Write to God asking Him to help you feel that same comfort and joy at home in Him. It is possible, but it won't come because you tried. It will come becuase you ask and rely on God to supply.

Write to God below -

James 1:17 Every good and perfect gift is from above, coming down from the Father of the heavenly lights, who does not change like shifting shadows.

Silent Night

Franz Gruber

Si - lent night, Ho - ly night!
Si - lent night, Ho - ly night!
Si - lent night, Ho - ly night!

All is calm, all is bright.
Shep - herds quake at the sight.
Son of God love's pure light.

Round yon Vir - gin, Moth - er and Child.
Glo - ries stream from heav - en a - far.
Ra - diant beams from Thy Ho - ly face.

Ho - ly in - fant so ten - der and mild,
Heav'n - ly hosts sing Al - le - lu - ia,
With the dawn of re - deem - ing grace,

Sleep in heav - en - ly peace,
Christ the Sav - ior is born!
Je - sus Lord, at Thy birth.

Sle - ep in heav - en - ly peace.
Christ the Sav - ior is born.
Je - sus Lord, at Thy birth.

©MichaelKravchuk.com

December 15

Silent night, Holy night. All is calm, all is bright.

Flooded with light. When we picture the first Holy night, we may picture it being dark and dimly lit. "All is bright" isn't the first thing that comes to mind. Sit with God in this. Consider some dark places in your life. Maybe it's a worry or an area that seems hopeless. Picture it in a dark place, maybe in a corner left alone. Ask God to break through the darkness and picture that corner being flooded with light. God is more powerful than darkness and His hope breaks through. Nothing is too dark for Him. It will likely not be fixed in an instant, but for those of us who call on His name, we are never alone in the dark. This may take practice, but any situation can feel calm and bright as we ask God to flood our situations with light and peace, much like we may picture Mary and Joseph sitting in on that Holy night.

For reflection - What are places in your life you need to be flooded with calm and light? Write to God asking Him to break through the darkness and flood the situation with light and peace. Consider what His response to you might be, believing He is close and cares for you.

Write to God below -

Ephesians 1:18 I pray that your hearts will be flooded with light so that you can understand the confident hope he has given to those he called. (NLT)

December 16

Round yon Virgin, Mother and Child. Holy Infant so tender and mild. Sleep in heavenly peace, sleep in heavenly peace.

Peace. Heavenly peace won't come just because our gifts are purchased or the shopping list and menu are prepared, but we sure live like that sometimes. Heavenly peace is sourced from the Lord. It is steady and unwavering. Close your eyes and picture God supplying your heart with heavenly peace. See it soothing the cracks and washing over your dry and tired places. Receive His heavenly peace.

For reflection - What tasks are you trying to complete in your own energy? How could you invite God into your to-do lists? Write to God and ask Him to join you and ask how you can join Him. Ask that streams of living water flow from within you. Did you hear a response from Him? If you didn't, keep asking.

Write to God below -

John 7:38 Whoever believes in me, as Scripture has said, rivers of living water will flow from within them.

December 17

Silent night, Holy night.
Shepherds quake at the sight.

Awe. Are your eyes fixated on the to-do lists, gifts to wrap or treats to bake? Take a moment and ask God for eyes to see. Ask God to stir awe at His plan of redemption, how He carried it to fulfillment and still does. Even as you feel tired working to make memories and foster joy, picture yourself sitting on a dark hill, watching over the fields as the shepherds did. Ask God to stir awe as you imagine what was happening in the little town just over the hill in Bethlehem on that Holy night.

For reflection - Consider being a shepherd in the field. What would you feel as you heard the angels in the dark of the night? What would you wonder? Ask God to compel your heart with awe in such a way that you too would leave your sheep and your to-do list in pursuit of Him.

Write to God below -

Luke 2:10-12 But the angel said to them,
"Do not be afraid. I bring you good news that will cause great joy for all the people. Today in the town of David a Savior has been born to you; he is the Messiah, the Lord. This will be a sign to you:
You will find a baby wrapped in cloths and lying in a manger."

December 18

Glories stream from heaven afar. Heavenly hosts sing, "Alleluia, Christ the Savior is born. Christ the Savior is born."

It's happening. Alleluia means God be praised. Imagine the angels singing. I wonder if when Jesus was born, the angels whispered in holy awe, "It's happening. God be praised. We've been waiting for so long, and it's happening." Sit in the picture. Watch the happenings and let your heart join the angels in their celebration and praise.

For reflection - Is there something you have been waiting to happen for a long time? Talk to God about that. Ask Him where He would like you to place your trust and anticipation. Ask Him to help you trust He knows best. Ask Him to take care of you while you wait.

Write to God below -

Proverbs 3:5-6 Trust in the LORD with all your heart
and lean not on your own understanding;
in all your ways submit to him, and he will make your paths straight.

December 19

Silent night, Holy night. Son of God love's pure light. Radiant beams from Thy holy face, with the dawn of redeeming grace. Jesus Lord, at Thy birth, Jesus Lord at Thy Birth.

Redeeming Grace. As God's children, we have received the redeeming grace of Jesus. Do you live as one who believes they are renewed and restored by redeeming grace? When Jesus is the King of our hearts, we can live redeemed and restored. Let this in. Believe that you are covered with His redeeming grace. Be redeemed by love's pure light.

For reflection - Does your life reflect that you have been set free by redeeming grace? Do you live as a slave to things God has already set you free from? What do you live as a slave to? Write those down and surrender them to God. God I surrender _____. God I seek to _____.
Ask Him to help you take in the truth that, like the dawn, your redeeming grace has come.

Write to God below -

Psalm 130:7 Israel, put your hope in the LORD,
for with the Lord is unfailing love and with him is full redemption.

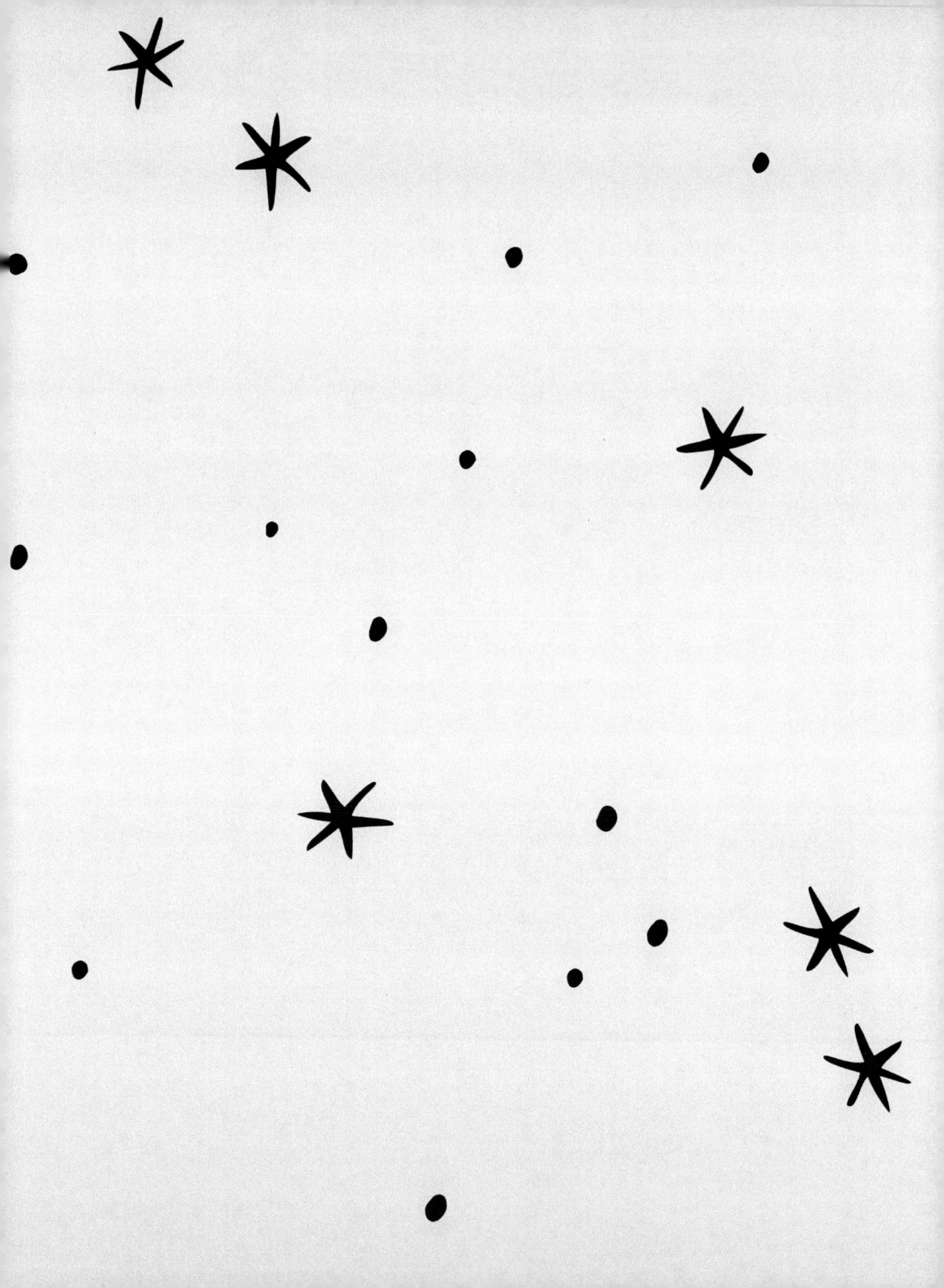

O Holy Night

Adolphe Charles Adams

O Ho-ly Night! The stars are bright-ly shi - ning, It is the night of our
Led by the light of faith se-rene-ly beam - ing, With glow-ing hearts by His
Tru-ly He taught us love for one a-noth - er, His law is love and His

dear Sav-iour's birth. Long lay the world in sin and er-ror pin -
cra-dle we stand. O - ver the world a star is sweet-ly gleam -
gos-pel is peace. Chains He shall break, the slave is our broth -

ning. Till He ap-peared and the soul felt its worth. A thrill of hope the
ing, Now come the wise-men from O - ri-ent land. The King of kings lay
er, And in His name all op-pres-sion shall cease. Sweet hymns of joy in

wea-ry world re-joi-ces, For yon-der breaks a new and glor-ious morn. Fall
thus in low-ly man-ger; In all our tri-als born to be our friend. He
grate-ful chor-us raise we, With all our hearts we praise His ho-ly name. Christ

on your knees! Oh, hear the an-gel voi - ces! O night
knows our need, our weak-ness is no strang - er! Be - hold
is the Lord! Oh, praise His name for-ev - er! His pow'r

di - vine, O night when Christ was born; O
your King! Be - fore him low-ly bend! Be -
and glo - ry ev - er - more pro-claim! His

night, O Ho - ly Night, O night di - vine!
hold your King! Be - fore Him low-ly bend!
pow'r and glo - ry ev - er - more pro - claim!

©MichaelKravchuk.com

December 20 ★

★ O Holy night, the stars are brightly shining.

When love broke through. Picture yourself in the country. You look around and the dark seems endless. You look up again and the sky is teeming with stars. As you look back down, the dark doesn't seem so dark anymore. On that holy night, when love broke through into the darkness, the world would never again be as dark. Light had come into the darkness. Ask God to help you picture light breaking through the darkness. Ask Him to give you eyes to see how that changed everything. Ask Him to see where that is still happening today.

For reflection - Ask God to give you eyes to see how everything changed when love broke through at Jesus' birth. How did everything change for the world? How did everything change for you on that holy night?

Write to God below -

John 8:12 When Jesus spoke again to the people, he said,
"I am the light of the world. Whoever follows me will never walk in darkness, but will have the light of life."

December 21

It is the night of our dear Savior's birth.

Our dear Savior. Spend some time picturing baby Jesus in the manger. Let the thought sink in, "That is my dear Savior." Stay with that thought. Set a five minute timer to stop and savor the picture of our Savior. As other things come into your mind, gently return to the place of, "That is my dear Savior."

For reflection - How did picturing baby Jesus in the manger as your Savior make you feel? What feelings did that stir up? Write them down. Did anything resonate in your heart? If not, that's okay, but give God the space so if He did want to say something, you could hear Him.

Write to God below -

Luke 2:4-7 So Joseph also went up from the town of Nazareth in Galilee to Judea, to Bethlehem the town of David, because he belonged to the house and line of David. He went there to register with Mary, who was pledged to be married to him and was expecting a child. While they were there, the time came for the baby to be born, and she gave birth to her firstborn, a son. She wrapped him in cloths and placed him in a manger, because there was no guest room available for them.

December 22

Long lay the world in sin and error pining, till he appear'd and the soul felt its worth.

The soul felt its worth. Do you remember what it was like the first time your soul felt its worth? It may be difficult to describe, but let's ask God to help us feel His love for us. It's as simple as asking, "God, could You give me a glimpse of Your love for me?" Then wait. "Help my soul feel its worth." It may be a moment in the day or something you hear Him speak to you. It may be a Bible passage that jumps off the page. As God's daughter, you are treasured and seen. If you are one He has revealed His Son to, you are chosen. Believe Him. Sit with God in that today, and may your soul feel its worth.

For reflection - What does it mean for your soul to feel its worth? Has there been a time when you felt seen by God? Ask God to show you that you are seen today. Look for Him everywhere. Come back to this and write about where you felt seen by God today.

Write to God below -

Ephesians 1:3-4 Praise be to the God and Father of our Lord Jesus Christ, who has blessed us in the heavenly realms with every spiritual blessing in Christ. For he chose us in him before the creation of the world to be holy and blameless in his sight.

December 23

The thrill of hope.

Hope. Anticipation. The feeling when your heart skips a beat at the thought of seeing someone you haven't seen for awhile or the feeling you get on Christmas morning as you walk down the stairs. The thrill of hope. Spend some time considering what anticipation feels like to you. Ask God to give you holy anticipation as you prepare to celebrate the coming of His Son. God, grant us the thrill of hope.

For reflection - What is something about the next couple of days you are eagerly anticipating? What are you most excited about? Write to God, asking Him for holy anticipation as you prepare to celebrate, then thank Him for the thrill of hope.

Write to God below -

Romans 15:13 May the God of hope fill you with all joy and peace as you trust in him, so that you may overflow with hope by the power of the Holy Spirit.

December 24

The weary world rejoices.

Rejoice. Rejoicing at the birth of Jesus isn't something I naturally do on my own. It may be natural for you, but I have to ask God to stir me to rejoice. Even after all the days of anticipation, we may think more about our family's Christmas Day than the Big Day in Bethlehem. Let's ask God to stir us awake and compel our souls to rejoice. Pause, sit with God. Set a five minute timer and intentionally rejoice. Tell Him about how thankful you are for Jesus and the redemption of your soul, transferring you from darkness to light. Sit with Him and let your heart rejoice.

For reflection - What would it look like for you to experience these next few days, not as a consumer, but as a worshiper? Write to God, asking Him to make the truth of Jesus' birth a reality in your heart that compels you to rejoice. Tell Him you want to live in awe of Him.

Write to God below -

Matthew 1:23 "The virgin will conceive and give birth to a son, and they will call him Immanuel" (which means "God with us").

December 25

For yonder breaks a new and glorious morn.

Glory. Picture the sunrise. When the sun peeks over the horizon and the sky fills with color, it's glorious. Light has come. We have asked God to prepare our hearts; now we welcome the new and glorious morn. Spend some time picturing the first peek of light over the horizon. Ask God to help your heart let in the reality that today we celebrate Jesus has come. The glorious light has come into the darkness. Jesus, God made man to rescue each of us. The birth of Jesus is for me. The birth of Jesus is for you. What a glorious morn.

For reflection - Do you feel like the birth of Jesus is for you? Talk with God about that. Ask Him to help you let that reality sink into your heart.

Write to God below -

John 1:14 The Word became flesh and made his dwelling among us. We have seen his glory, the glory of the one and only Son, who came from the Father, full of grace and truth.

December 26

Fall on your knees. O hear the angel voices. O night divine.

Worship. Jesus is the Messiah. Jesus is the Savior of the world. Jesus is your Messiah. Jesus is the Savior of you. Jesus is our Messiah. He is the Savior of me.

For reflection - Write this down: Jesus is the Messiah. Jesus is the Savior of the world. Jesus is my Messiah. Jesus is the Savior of me. How will you let this reality change you? How will you go forward with Jesus the King of your heart?

Write to God below -

Isaiah 9:6 For to us a child is born, to us a son is given, and the government will be on his shoulders.
And he will be called Wonderful Counselor, Mighty God, Everlasting Father, Prince of Peace.

John 1:14 The Word became flesh and made his dwelling among us. We have seen his glory, the glory of the one and only Son, who came from the Father, full of grace and truth.

Thank you for journeying with us this Christmas. You may be asking what's next. To stay in the know on our future projects, follow @holdlooselylivefreely. You will also find additional resources as you look to grow your faith at ifgathering.com.

If you have felt God calling your heart this season, He likely is. Keep looking for Him. We believe He has a specific purpose for your life and that you will find it as you listen for His voice and do what He says. You can learn to hear Him by reading His Word and praying, asking Him for the things that you need. Keep making the space and staying centered on the way, the truth, and the life. The centered life is the best life, for today and for forever.

Made in the USA
Coppell, TX
03 December 2022